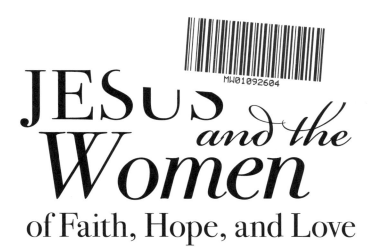

JESUS *and the* *Women*

of Faith, Hope, and Love

Sergio
Stevan

Liguori
LIGUORI, MISSOURI

Dedication

Those who in the Church
follow the Gospel from close up
light lamps of faith,
guard reserves of hope, and
feed the fire of love.

Imprimi Potest: Harry Grile, CSsR
Provincial, Denver Province, The Redemptorists

First published in the United States by Liguori Publications
Liguori, Missouri 63057
To order, call 800-325-9521, or visit liguori.org

The original Italian, *Al re piacerà la tua bellezza,* by Sergio Stevan, copyright © 2009
Libreria Editrice Vaticana

English translation copyright © 2011 Liguori Publications

Library of Congress Cataloging-in-Publication
Stevan, Sergio.
 Jesus and the women of faith, hope, and love / Sergio Stevan.—1st ed.
  p. cm.
 ISBN 978-0-7648-2027-4
 1. Mary Magdalene, Saint—Meditations. 2. Bible. N.T. John XX, 1–18—Meditations. 3.
Mary, of Bethany, Saint—Meditations. 4. Bible. N.T. Luke VII, 36-50—Meditations. 5.
Bible. N.T. John XII, 1–8—Meditations. I. Title.
 BS2485.S7313 2011
 226'.092082—dc22
            2011000111

Scripture citations are taken from the *New Revised Standard Version* of the Bible,
copyright 1989 by the Division of Christian Education of the National Council of
Churches of Christ in the USA. All rights reserved. Used with permission.

This book was translated from the original Italian, *Al re piacerà la tua bellezza,*
by Father Russell Abata, CSsR.

Liguori Publications, a nonprofit corporation, is an apostolate of the Redemptorists.
To learn more about the Redemptorists, visit Redemptorists.com.

Printed in the United States of America
15 14 13 12 11   5 4 3 2 1

First Edition

Contents

Preface   6

Introduction   8

Mary Magdalene:
THE SHOUT OF FAITH   11

The Pardoned Sinner:
THE COURAGE OF HOPE   20

Mary of Bethany:
THE MIRACLE OF LOVE   31

Appendix 1
THE PENITENT MAGDALENE   39

Appendix 2
WOMEN AT THE SERVICE OF THE GOSPEL   43

Preface

"O Mother of life,
we of every generation call you blessed.
O beautiful Spouse,
Divinely accepted by the immortal Father,
O receptacle of the divine Paraclete,
O Mother of the King of glory,
mirror of love, eternal Beauty—
The whole course of your life is engulfed
with blessedness."

So sings the Recluse Neophyte about Mary, Our Lady, and in this song is echoed the beauty of blessedness that adorns every woman committed to mystery.

Ancient wisdom has always united beauty with eros in a reciprocal, fascinating relationship. Beauty arouses love, and love informs beauty in an unending dialogue.

"You are the most handsome of men; grace is poured upon your lips; therefore God has blessed you for ever," affirms Psalm 45:2 as it describes the wedding of the king. In Christ is guarded that power of beauty that is capable of inspiring, motivating, transforming, and modeling human life. It is the beauty of the fully, who has trusted her, who has restored her dignity and made her feel truly loved.

The sinner is received by Jesus without being judged. He knows her in a profound way, and he knows what she really needs. "She has finally found in Jesus a pure eye, a heart capable of loving without exploiting her. In the look and heart of Jesus are revealed that God is love!" (Benedict XVI, homily, June 17, 2007)

The pardoned sinner is a symbol of a hope that no longer permits her to say: "There is nothing I can do, I am not able to change." Her repentance allows grace to touch her heart and restores her capacity to love God, her neighbor, and herself.

Before his passion, Jesus went to Bethany to the house of his special friends Martha, Mary, and Lazarus. Jesus sat at table with them, suffering in silence and consumed by thought, and yet was not understood by his friends. Only Mary sensed that even at this meal with his friends, Jesus was afflicted with a great sadness. For this reason she boldly poured perfumed oil on the feet of Jesus. This fragrance, the perfume of love, cannot be bought or sold. It can only be given away.

Where love is growing, faith, hope, and joy flower at the same time. Mary of Nazareth, the Mother of Jesus, contains in herself the roots of these three virtues. The source of her steps on this journey of faith is an exuberant response to the love in her life.

The angel of the Lord enters and Mary is filled with grace. Love makes space, and the woman of Nazareth is embraced by warmth. To believe is to accept each new step of the mystery of God encountering his creature.

Where faith arises, love flows. Love enters, faith receives, love overflows. Mary sets out on the journey to meet her cousin Elizabeth "in haste" (Luke 1:39) because she does not need to think about it. She is ready to begin the adventure of love and to share it with others. The fruit of love is love given and received.

The baby in the womb of Elizabeth leaps because it is clear to him that love is at the door. John's movement is full of strength and hope; it is a hymn of joy.

The steps of Mary tell of her encounter with love. The fruit of this encounter are faith, hope, and charity. Outside of this encounter with love, the three theological virtues are illusions, like sterile fruits on the tree of life.

The spirit of the Lord, who always arouses in the heart of the disciple the desire to be like Jesus, accompanies us in the walk with him. The abundant and surprising fruits of Gospel virtues mature among the leaves of our poor lives.

Mary Magdalene
THE SHOUT OF FAITH

*T*he word of God is the answer to all problems...even to those that appear to be incomprehensible, beyond repair, unjust. The word of God is the compass of our life.

"Early on the first day of the week, while it was still dark, Mary Magdalene came to the tomb and saw that the stone had been removed from the tomb. So she ran and went to Simon Peter and the other disciple, the one whom Jesus loved, and said to them, 'They have taken the Lord out of the tomb, and we do not know where they have laid him'" (John 20:1–2).

"But Mary stood weeping outside the tomb. As she wept, she bent over to look into the tomb; and she saw two angels in white, sitting where the body of Jesus had been lying, one at the head and the other at the feet. They said to her, 'Woman, why are you weeping?' She said to them, 'They have taken away my Lord, and I do not know where they have laid him.' When she had said this, she turned round and saw Jesus standing there, but she did not know that it was Jesus. Jesus said to her, 'Woman, why are you weeping? For whom are you looking?' Supposing him to be the gardener, she said to him, 'Sir, if you have carried him away, tell me where you have laid him, and I

will take him away.' Jesus said to her, 'Mary!' She turned and said to him in Hebrew, 'Rabbouni!' (which means Teacher). Jesus said to her, 'Do not hold on to me, because I have not yet ascended to the Father. But go to my brothers and say to them, "I am ascending to my Father and your Father, to my God and your God."' Mary Magdalene went and announced to the disciples, 'I have seen the Lord'; and she told them that he had said these things to her" (John 20: 11–18).

Close to the tomb

Finally the dawn of Sunday came. Mary, dragged down by the events of Friday, aimlessly wanders to the tomb.

She is a woman walking ever so slowly. Depressed, she goes toward the dullness of the day with death in her heart and wrapped in a profound sadness.

Mary cannot help but go. She cannot do anything less. Love pushes her to the tomb. She goes to repay the Lord for what she has received—liberation from seven demons. She goes looking for a dead body to give it a fitting gesture of attention and to honor her teacher and her Lord.

For Mary Magdalene, who loves Jesus more than any other, it is still night.

Night! It is the test of faith. In the Gospel of John we read that when Judas left the room of the last supper it was still night (John 13:30).

She goes to the tomb while it is still night, but not knowing it, she is heading toward the light of dawn.

Having arrived at the tomb, she sees with horror that the rock blocking the tomb has been rolled away, and the body of Jesus is gone.

Mary feels faint. All of the tension of waiting falls on her like a block of concrete. She sits on a rock and cries.

Tears

She stood there disfigured by tears.

Mary Magdalene is a woman who knows how to cry from the emptiness one experiences after the loss of a friend, from a failure, from grief.

Perhaps in these circumstances there are those who would always like to appear strong, who are able to take it all like a virtuous ascetic, like irreproachable persons who by sheer might must always win, who are more preoccupied with their own perfection than with that of God.

But the power of God also passes through the vulnerability of humans. It is not always easy to be able to stand in the midst of others with the courage of fragility.

It is a great gift to know how to cry with those who cry. We read in the life of Saint Ambrose who "rejoiced with those who were joyful, cried with those afflicted. Every time someone confessed his sins to him to receive the penance, he cried so much that he reduced the penitent to tears. In fact, he considered himself a sinner among sinners."

The cry of others should never leave us tranquil. It should shake us and leave us questioning ourselves. When a person discovers and accepts his faults, in that moment he is able to be an instrument of the power of God. Even if he suffers being weak and inadequate, all the same he is content because he rediscovers himself every day as a sinner, while in his heart grace is at work. It is truly in weakness that the presence and power of God is revealed.

They have taken away my Lord

Suddenly, two angels appear. They ask her, "Woman, why are you crying?" She answered, "They have taken away my Lord..." The reason for her tears is because she has lost someone who gave her security. Magdalene lives a torturous searching of the night. She has found the tomb empty and does not know how to believe or how to respond to the angels. She is living the experience of a woman in love who has lost her loved one.

Mary does not recognize the Lord. She is weary from that walk of faith that passes through the darkness of the night where "she does not see." She has felt the painful absence of the Lord.

Mary loses the knowledge of belonging to someone. She loses the deepest sense of her life and support.

She cries because that point of support that redeemed her and made her feel as a woman has weakened.

Mary Magdalene was a "used" woman; Jesus has loved her and accepted her as she was and has loved her, despite allegations that she was a prostitute.

God loves us because he finds us fragile and so needy of everything. Anyone who seriously walks with Jesus lives the experience of his absence.

Mary cries because she no longer feels loved, and for this reason she is more of a corpse than the Jesus she seeks. But Mary's cries are born from the discovery of a truth. It is a weeping that is healing and saving. It is a gift of tears and conversion.

Jesus, Mary of Bethany, and Peter have all cried. They have cried tears of love.

We can ask why Peter, after his denial and repentance, did not follow Jesus to the top of Calvary. Perhaps he preferred to stay with himself and with his tears. To cry alone is dangerous because one is able to close in on oneself.

Crying expresses different things. Tears were seen as a sign of weakness, but they are a mysterious manner of communicating. One cries when it is no longer possible to hold together a sense of life. At times the cry of our brothers disturbs our life. Faced with the tears of others, we can be indifferent or we can mock them.

Jesus, what place do you occupy in my life?
For whom am I searching?

How am I searching for the Lord in the midst of my tears?
Why I am crying?

In front of whom am I crying?

Behind the tears of this woman there is restlessness trying to make sense of things.

The angels ask her, "Why are you crying?" And Jesus asks, "Who are you seeking?" It is this last question that is so profound because it forces us to seriously reflect.

Mary cries before the Lord, even if she does not recognize him. "Woman, why are your crying? For whom are you looking?" Jesus wants what really is in the heart of this woman to emerge. He not only questions her but leads her to the answer.

"You are looking for someone, who do you seek, who do you depend on?" She responds, "They have carried off my Lord and I do not know where they have placed him." "My Lord" is an expression that is applied to a loved one. Hers is a response full of love.

Mary turns, sees Jesus standing there, and does not recognize him. Jesus invites her to escape from the slavery of her past, and he calls her by name.

"Mary!" She feels again recognized and loved. Mary's joy is full. An unforeseen peace, after so much suffering, descends into her soul. The weight that oppressed her heart rolls away like the stone of the tomb. The man who has called her by name approaches her. She, at first not believing her own ears, suddenly falls to her knees and, sobbing with joy, she shouts, "Rabbouni!"

The master has returned. He is there with her. He calls her. He has not abandoned her!

Thus ends the torturous waiting. The fear and uncertainty of tomorrow dissolves.

Do not touch me

Mary wants to cling to Jesus, but he tells her, "Do not detain me because I am not only yours, but go to my brothers and tell them, 'I ascend to my Father.'"

Even though her desire to remain with the Lord is strong, Mary left him with secure and decisive steps. She rises and goes with a new heart to seek out the disciples and tell them all that has happened.

The voice and the glance

The hope of Mary Magdalene to find her Lord again did not ever decrease, even though with pain she had to pass through the desert of loneliness.

It was enough that she recognized the voice calling her name, that she felt filled with a presence that does not leave space for pain or sadness. The gift of two glances that were shared was enough for her to feel found and loved.

"Jesus said to her, 'Mary'" (John 20:16). "After he called her with the generic name of her gender, 'Woman,' without being recognized, he calls her by name, as if he wanted to say, 'You recognized the one who has recognized you. I know you not as one recognizes any person, but in a way that is totally special.' Mary, then, called by name, recognizes her Creator and suddenly shouts, 'Rabbouni,' that is 'Teacher.' It was he who she looked for exteriorly, and it was he who guided her interiorly in the search" (Saint Gregory the Great).

For the first time in her life, she has found someone who has understood her completely, who has trusted her. He has given back her dignity and finally made her feel loved.

> *"Anyone who wishes to give love must also receive love as a gift" (Benedict XVI,* Deus caritas est, *n. 7).*

I have seen the Lord

Mary Magdalene quickly accepts the request of the Lord and goes to say, "I have seen the Lord!"

Her eyes are open.

The announcement of the resurrection explodes in a most convincing way because it gushes from a heart that is in love.

When one seriously loves God, she has only one desire: to make God known and loved. Mary Magdalene's shout is not only the communication of an event but the announcement of a joy that comes from an encounter with the Lord.

Mary Magdalene's joy is a song of life for everyone.

The spiritual experience of this woman is a great help for us. She has lived sadness and desperation, but after the encounter with Jesus she is able to announce that the experience of faith is always possible and is rewarded despite pain and death. After the blackness of the night, God also calls each one of us by our name. Mary Magdalene is a sign of faith in the risen Lord.

Faith is alive when the believer experiences that the God who created her, loves her, and feels that love when God searches for her.

Without a personal encounter with Jesus, faith is dormant. It is only Jesus who can send us to announce that we have seen him.

The risen Jesus is not to be selfishly clung to, but announced and given to others.

> *"Union with Christ is also union with all those to whom he gives himself. I cannot possess Christ just for myself; I can belong to him only in union with all those who have become, or who will become, his own"*
> *(Benedict XVI,* Deus caritas est, *n. 14).*

Is there a passion in me to want to announce Christ to others?

Do I bring the Lord to others, not as something that belongs to me, but as a gift I have been given?

In each of us can exist the double experience—tears and joy. Sadness and melancholy are the true enemies of joy. Pain is not. It makes joy strong and profound. It makes joy active.

Reflection

I have come to you, Jesus,
to feel your touch
throughout my days.
Let your eyes rest in mine for awhile
that I can bring into my work
the security of your friendship.
Fill my mind
So that it can endure across
the wilderness of noise.
Make it so that only your blessing
fills the heights of my thoughts,
and give me the strength to serve
all who need me.
Amen.

—Blessed Teresa of Calcutta

The Pardoned Sinner
THE COURAGE OF HOPE

"*One of the Pharisees asked Jesus to eat with him, and he went into the Pharisee's house and took his place at the table. And a woman in the city, who was a sinner, having learned that he was eating in the Pharisee's house, brought an alabaster jar of ointment. She stood behind him at his feet, weeping, and began to bathe his feet with her tears and to dry them with her hair. Then she continued kissing his feet and anointing them with the ointment. Now when the Pharisee who had invited him saw it, he said to himself, 'If this man were a prophet, he would have known who and what kind of woman this is who is touching him—that she is a sinner.' Jesus spoke up and said to him, 'Simon, I have something to say to you.' 'Teacher,' he replied, 'speak.' 'A certain creditor had two debtors; one owed five hundred denarii, and the other fifty. When they could not pay, he cancelled the debts for both of them. Now which of them will love him more?' Simon answered, 'I suppose the one for whom he cancelled the greater debt.' And Jesus said to him, 'You have judged rightly.' Then turning towards the woman, he said to Simon, 'Do you see this woman? I entered your house; you gave me no water for my feet, but she has bathed my feet with her tears and dried them with her hair. You gave me no kiss, but from the time I came in she has not stopped kissing my feet. You did not anoint my head with oil, but she has anointed my feet with ointment. Therefore, I tell you, her sins, which were many, have been forgiven; hence she has shown great love. But the one to whom little is forgiven, loves little"' (Luke 7: 36–47).*

Tears of repentance

The leading actors and persons of this scene are Jesus, Simon the Pharisee, the sinful woman, the disciples, and all of the other dinner guests.

We can also consider ourselves part of the scene because every time we find ourselves before a page of sacred Scripture we are involved and questioned.

This extract from the Gospel can appear a bit scandalous, but we can learn much from it. Our understanding is as clear as our patience and ability to interiorize the lessons of the story.

Let us get close to Jesus, who was invited to the dinner given by Simon the Pharisee in his house. The welcoming gestures of hospitality are gestures of generosity.

A woman in that city who everyone knows to be a sinner enters this wealthy house that is not hers.

It would be interesting to know what the other guests thought of her, and, in general, what we think of this woman. One could say that she is a "loose woman," but what is known about this woman? What has she had to suffer or face in her lifetime?

Before forming a judgment about a person, it is necessary to ask oneself what is known about her and her past. In that case, it is probable to find oneself worse than she.

Jesus, without judging her, accepts her because he knows her deeply and knows what she really needs.

> *"She has finally found in Jesus a pure eye, a heart capable of loving without exploiting her. In the look and heart of Jesus are revealed that God is Love!" (Benedict XVI, homily, June 17, 2007)*

In this woman is found a woman who cries, not because of the loss of a dear one. She cries tears of joy, tears of liberation of repentance and conversion that become a kind of baptismal font.

Because this woman previously has sinned so greatly, many look on her unkindly and are filled with prejudice. She is seen as an intruder, one who makes others feel embarrassed.

Am I perhaps among those people who with great ease make superficial judgments about others without fully understanding their situations?

But for some time now Jesus has been expecting her. She has the courage to demonstrate a new gesture of extraordinary and most exquisite love.

She washes the feet of Jesus with her tears and dries them with her hair. To wash the feet of another is an honorable courtesy.

Seeing this, the Pharisee began to judge the woman critically. Thanks to the Gospel it is possible to enter into the thoughts of this Pharisee.

He makes two judgments—one about the woman and one about Jesus. He decides that Jesus is not a prophet and the woman is a sinner.

The first judgment he makes is about Jesus. He thinks he cannot be a prophet because he would know "who she is, and the kind of woman who is touching him." The second is about the sinfulness of the woman.

Only Jesus knows the thoughts of the judgmental Pharisee and only Jesus, who has not judged this woman, can say truthfully what kind of woman she is. Jesus says, "Simon, I have something to say to you."

Teacher, tell me truthfully

Even though he makes the suppositions within himself, the Pharisee does not have the courage to say out loud what he is thinking.

Because of this, Simon the Pharisee was addressed by Jesus, "I have something to say to you."

Simon has allowed into his house a woman of ill repute, and he has not insulted her except within his mind. Even as Jesus questions him, he maintains an attitude toward her that is deferent, respectful, and friendly, all the time keeping his thoughts to himself.

He says to Jesus, "Tell me truly. I am here to listen to you."

Jesus, using a teaching method all his own, speaks to him with a parable about one who is owed money. He does not expose his words in a direct way, but he seeks to make his message understood by way of the people in the parable.

To paraphrase, "A lender forgives the debts of two people who owe him money—one five hundred units of money, the other fifty. Which of them would love him more?" Simon answers correctly and Jesus appreciated his answer, but he did not understand that Jesus was talking about him, and that the parable was turned back on him.

Simon does not hide. He realizes that his life is divided between what he thinks and feels and what he does. His ways are two worlds that do not meet. He lives in two ways. In the first he speaks only proper, cordial words to others. But inside, he is consumed by thoughts and judgments.

At heart Simon is a man who does not reconcile the two ways of living. He does not open himself to the reception of the Word of God because Simon does not see how Jesus' manner of reasoning applies to his life.

> *"It is one thing to know that God exists, another to know God" (Saint Silouan the Athonite).*

It is one thing to know that one is speaking with Jesus in the words of a prayer, another to know that he reads the heart and knows well all that a person does in life.

When he is with others, he is considered friendly and attentive; this allows him to more easily make judgments about others. In other words, the Pharisee has much he would like to teach others. He is content with the appearance of moral education, even while he has an interior life that is superficial and incapable of connecting what he believes with how he acts.

The parable of the Pharisee and the Publican helps us to perceive the same thing in ourselves.

With delicate and subtle determination, Jesus begins to enter the heart of Simon to help him discover that he has judged only by appearances.

In fact, he only knows she is a prostitute and does not even know the name of this woman kneeling at the feet of Jesus.

Jesus appears to want to say, "You are all appearance and judge others by appearances! Try to look at the interior of her personality and study her gestures. Try to consider with clarity that which is behind the actions of this woman and you will see that you are able to discover another truth. She is a sinful woman, but she is also repentant."

This woman has already changed her heart. She is already detached from that which she loved inordinately, and she already has found the only true love. "What have you done for me? You did not give me water, but she has bathed my feet with her tears and has dried them with her hair and has kissed them. Not only that, she has given me much more. She has given me her heart!"

It is here that the true conversion begins. "You did not give me a kiss (a sign of hospitality and welcome). She instead from when I arrived has not ceased to kiss my feet."

All of the affection, her expressions of love which at one time were put to the service of sin, now are redeemed, and this love is what saves.

The Lord saves her even though she has committed sin and makes us understand the truth she is seeking, even at the root of her sin.

The prostitute, in the erroneous use of her body, searched for the satisfaction of a great need, that of being loved.

Is there a conviction in us that in the depth of every sin there is always a desire for good?

Am I ready to give credit to this "depth of goodness" and work to redeem it and make it emerge, when it is possible, in the life of others?

Jesus does not reveal to others that which is apparent to the eyes of most people, and he does not obligate us to a total change. Through her sin he makes her understand the root of evil and thus finds the way to free herself from sin. "For this reason I tell you, her many sins are forgiven because she has loved much."

Who loves little

Those who receive little pardon love only a little. This forgiveness is not only a forgiveness that God gives, it is also a forgiveness that is required for love.

Simon the Pharisee is a man capable of a little love, and he is incapable of realizing that his great sin is his insensitive judgment.

A person capable of love, even if he errs in his choice of objects to love, always has the possibility to change himself. He can always orient his heart to the true good. On the contrary, a person who does not know how to love is hardhearted and does not give anything to anyone. He never lets himself be indebted to anyone.

It is better to have a heart bent over from errors than one that is cold and incapable of loving.

Someone, perhaps, does not err because he never places himself in conditions where it can happen. Simon the Pharisee, and this is the problem of the Pharisees, is not a bad person. He is faithful to the obligations of the Law, but he holds himself too erect. He is a person of granite, too secure.

When he is aware of committing a grave error and has the courage to let the heavy crust he has created around him drop, then he can begin his conversion.

Simon has put himself in a position of superiority in regard to Jesus, and he shows some annoyance because he has not received any gratitude for the invitation he has given to his house. Instead, this "horror" of a woman has received it all.

In this Gospel story we need to look at two levels: the heart of the Pharisee and the heart of the woman.

The heart of the Pharisee is restricted, narrow, insensitive, empty.

On the other hand, the heart of the woman is of the highest sentiment and most profound sincerity; the deepest experiences of gratitude, sorrow, and joy.

It is better to be sensitive with the risk of erring than present one's self as sinless but with a heart of stone.

At times the Lord uses the cracks of our sins as the only way to enter into the depths of our hearts.

With empty hands

The pardoned sinner is a symbol of hope which can no longer allow the person to say, "For me there is nothing I can do, so I can never change."

It is one who is penitent who allows grace to touch her heart and is able to recover her capacity to love God, neighbor, and self.

In the deepest part of her heart, she is a woman capable of love—a purified love.

On the other hand, Simon the Pharisee does not have the capacity to love.

We find this truth also in the parable of the prodigal son. The older brother does not leave home because he is unable to transgress even the smallest rule, but after a time he finds himself at a distance from his father's house because he would not even know where to run away.

This individual becomes a wretched person. He reproaches his father for not being given a kid goat to have a feast with his friends. Because of jealousy, he is not able to share his father's joy over the return of his brother.

He is wretched and miserly while the younger man who left and spent all he had realizes the errors he has committed and turns back his steps, repentant and pardoned.

In this way, this woman returns home pardoned and wrapped in a future of hope that opens up in front of her. We do not know how the Pharisee turned out after the invitation given to him by Jesus. Probably he is more shut down by way of his defenses and his proud presumptions.

Hope is the capacity to believe that even in the depths of sin the Lord knows how to give us the prospect of a new life. Putting herself at the feet of Jesus and recognizing her sins, and knowing that all of them have been touched by the Lord and grasped by him, she obtains salvation.

Paradoxically, it is better to travel a wrong road than to have the false certainty of traveling fast on a road she believes is right.

The Lord asks us to open our eyes and not have a fear of fragility and poverty and to maintain this attitude before him.

Saint Thérèse of Lisieux, in her act of offering herself to the merciful love of God with simplicity and profound intuition, wrote, "In the evening of this life, I will come before you with empty hands because I do not ask you, Lord, to count my works."

It certainly costs to have empty hands. We would rather present ourselves with hands full of the things we have done.

"I also see in regards to the present life it is vain to have hope...In regards to it there are obligations and expectations that are functional and passing. Hopes are for eternity" (Paul VI, Thoughts About Death*).*

The rehabilitated sinner helps us to believe in the virtue of hope, a virtue so little appreciated in our day.

And yet there is a great need for hope. Hope is not born from us but is a gift. It is from the Lord.

It makes us peaceful to hear, day after day, about people loved by the Lord, and who are certain that all we receive—from the air we breathe to the bread we eat, to the pardon we receive—all comes from this love. All, including the conversion of the heart, is a gift of God.

Do I try to cultivate actively and concretely the seeds of hope that the Spirit has placed in me?

Do I practice concrete gestures of trusting God, committing myself into his hands, when I am in real situations of poverty and trouble?

Reflection

Lord Jesus,
I am poor, as you are,
I am weak, as you are,
I am human, as you are.
All of my grandeur comes from your smallness,
My every force from your weakness,
All of my wisdom, from your foolishness!
I run toward you, O Lord,
Who heals the infirm,
gives strength to the weak,
Returns joy to the heart immersed in sadness...
I will follow you, Lord Jesus.
Amen.

SAINT AELRED OF RIEVAULX

Mary of Bethany
THE MIRACLE OF LOVE

"*ix days before the Passover Jesus came to Bethany, the home of Lazarus, whom he had raised from the dead. There they gave a dinner for him. Martha served, and Lazarus was one of those at the table with him. Mary took a pound of costly perfume made of pure nard, anointed Jesus' feet, and wiped them with her hair. The house was filled with the fragrance of the perfume. But Judas Iscariot, one of his disciples (the one who was about to betray him), said, 'Why was this perfume not sold for three hundred denarii and the money given to the poor?' (He said this not because he cared about the poor, but because he was a thief; he kept the common purse and used to steal what was put into it.) Jesus said, 'Leave her alone. She bought it so that she might keep it for the day of my burial. You always have the poor with you, but you do not always have me'" (John 12:1–8).*

Alone among his friends

It is right to approach this Gospel story with a kind of shame because we are at a scene of intimacy. We almost need to stay at its threshold with sincere openness of the heart, ready to contemplate rather than to comprehend, because love is not so much to understand but to live.

This passage, which comes right before the passion of Jesus, is a scene in Bethany. We meet Martha, a person who is attentive and dutiful, Lazarus, a personality of great significance because he has recently been brought back to life and is the focus of attention of the curious dinner guests, and Jesus who sits at table. He is intimately alone. There are only six days before his passion, before his Easter.

In his experience of loneliness, even though he is in a house of his friends, where he is able to rest and feel welcomed, Jesus feels the weariness of being human. He knows that his enemies are plotting against him. Many do not understand him because they are unable to read what is written in his heart.

As he sits at table, it does not seem like an ordinary day. There is an air of celebration. But Jesus is living a most painful kind of solitude. He suffers in silence without being understood. He is not able to turn to anyone, not because of ill will but from their lack of understanding. He seems unable to express himself.

The fact that he is in a festive setting makes his solitude even more intense. In these moments a good word is expected, but no one is capable of offering such a gift. It is even probable that another does not even imagine the torment locked in the heart of his friend.

It can happen that behind secure attitudes are hidden great tragedies that reveal themselves in unforeseen ways, leaving those outside profoundly affected.

Jesus lives his loneliness without fear of revealing his need for others. In fact in the Garden of Olives he asks, "Stay awake with me."

The greatness of Jesus is not that he hides his suffering but that he seeks his disciples to remain with him. This is a teaching that shows us how to live in difficult circumstances. One runs two risks. One is to continuously pity ourselves, and the other is to close in on ourselves while shutting out others.

Jesus in the Garden distances himself a stone's throw from his friends to be alone with his solitude, but at the same time be able to seek their company. It is a balance in which he does not close in on himself and at the same time he is able to have enough space to maintain a distance and to seek help in the right way.

Am I able to conduct myself in a mature way and be aware of my solitude?

Do I allow myself to be swallowed up by solitude or to run away from my loneliness in a frantic search for support?

Love does not die

We return to our scene. The most important character here is Mary. Here we must acknowledge the sensitivity of women—only a woman can perceive the solitude of Jesus. Only a woman can see and understand what he really needs.

Charity and love alone place her in this intuitive situation. Even Martha loves the Lord, but it is Mary who has perceived that, beyond the feast, Jesus has a different need. She intuits that Jesus is assailed by a profound sadness.

With the gesture of pouring a perfumed oil on the feet of Jesus, Mary shakes up all who are present and disturbs the climate of the meal. Mary's is an unexpected gesture. As is ordinary, she washes the feet of the guest, but in pouring the perfumed oil on the feet of Jesus, she does something that seems exaggerated and almost foolish.

One knows that love is also foolishness. Her gesture seems foolish because of the waste, but even more foolish seems Mary's boldness.

Pouring the perfume is really a sign of waste, of loss, a gesture with no gain. The perfume is the most precious thing the woman has, but she is consumed with pure love, the giving of a pure gift, not to men, but to God.

This gesture for one who is not contemplative is a disjointed one, useless and without sense. She pours a precious perfume of pure nard. It is all of the riches she possesses, and it is a gift without seeking self-interest, all for the Lord.

Mary is a free woman who is capable of loving. In fact, if a person is not free interiorly, she is not capable of loving.

"There is need of only one thing" (Luke 10:42), Mary was heard to say...She gave what she had, her most precious possession.

The small jar filled with perfume is the price of a soul that gives without making many calculations.

Am I capable, have I ever been capable of gratuitous gestures of love for the Lord?

Am I capable of these bold gestures that express my profound desire to give myself to God?

The woman is great because she has given everything, and she has done it in a delicate way.

When one gives all, even if it is a little, and it is given with generosity and without much calculation, there is no loss, but only gain. It is no longer a death, but a life because it was done with love.

Love therefore is a delivery, a total gift, a giving of one's self, a death...

The figure of Mary who listens to the Word of God seated at the feet of Jesus, Mary who sits in the house in wait for others who come to console her over the death of her brother, Lazarus, this is the same Mary who is capable of giving all to listen to Jesus, both pain and love.

Her perfume is really like love. It spills over and becomes apostolic, uniting everyone. It moves and is recorded forever. It will continue over the centuries, because when love is authentic it travels, is not lost, is outside of time, lives on forever. Love does not die even if the person who has performed the gesture is no more.

The wonders of perfume

The aroma of the perfume is a sign of the feast. It unites all who are in the house, those who could enter but do not, those who are expected but do not arrive. It is a perfume that penetrates everywhere, in the clothing, in the surroundings and unites everyone, just like Christian love.

It is necessary that the encounter with the Lord be this way until love reaches its fullness and becomes communicable.

People today have a hunger and thirst for a tenderness that is given by a disinterested heart, by a heart rich with love.

What are the needs of those who are desperate, who live alone without friends, who feel the weight of the oppression of guilt? Certainly such a one has need of the gift of tenderness, of delicacy, of the subtleties of the heart, of closeness and of small gestures, and the highest kind of attention that come to the person as sweet and delightful music.

There is need of this delicacy, this attraction of the perfume of love that involves all persons. This perfume stopped its course before the heart of Judas, the egotist and calculator.

He will stop it more in the upper room when he will leave banging the door, showing himself definitely for who he is: the traitor.

"Why was this perfume not sold for three hundred day's wages and given to the poor?"

Judas expresses a typical question, one that has nothing to do with the poor, because when in the name of poverty one tramples on charity, as Judas has, he offends and does not serve the truth.

The perfume cannot be sold. It can only be offered.

Blinded Judas was lacking in love. The gesture of the woman is annoying to him, not so much for the waste but because of the intensity of the love in her that he could not fathom.

Every gesture of love annoys him, irritates him, makes him aggressive. He is a man who is troubled, greedy, a slave, and a thief. The poor are not important to him. He holds the purse and takes what others place in it. On the other hand, the woman gives her perfume graciously to show her love.

Does it happen to me that perhaps I am irritated because of love?

The absence of Jesus

Judas uses the poor to cover up his uneasiness.

Jesus uses with ease the beautiful expression, "Let her do it... The poor, in fact, you have always with you, but you will not always have me."

Certainly the poor will never be lacking, especially as we, ourselves, are often the poor.

The problem is that "you will not always have me!" Jesus says. Let us imagine the experience of the absence of God. We know there are seasons where the Lord lets himself be found and other seasons where he is hidden, and we live the weariness of faith, and hope seems far away.

What are the things that have made the mystics of the Church great? Saint John of the Cross, Saint Teresa of Avila, Saint Thérèse of Lisieux, the Blessed Mother Teresa of Calcutta? What thing has sustained the faith of these saints? They were not able to feel, nor see, nor touch God but were willing to love him with boldness. This gives testimony that real love is gratuitous, seeking only God and not the benefits that come from him.

In silence, we can enter into contemplation, hear the music of God's love, savor the scent of this love.

The love we are attaining to we draw from the cross, the great sign of love. Only our promise to walk in love purifies us and makes us creatures who can testify to the love of God.

Our walk in love should become visible because our joy and happiness have their roots in love.

The Lord in baptism has given us, as Pope Benedict XVI, quoting Saint Gregory the Great, said, the "vestment of light." This is the vestment of love. "A person without love is darkness inside. The external darkness, of which the Gospel speaks, is only the reflection of the internal blindness of the heart" (Benedict XVI, homily of the Mass of Chrism, 2007).

Reflection

If I lift up to you, my God, my shout of love,
I do not do it for the heaven you have promised me;
Nor to distance myself from the terrors of hell.
But I love you, my God, contemplating you this way,
Nailed to the cross purple with your blood.
I love your wounds and your death,
I love your love.
Beyond your gifts and your promises,
Even if there were no heaven or hell,
I know, my God, that I would love you the same.
To love you is for me more happiness than obligation.
Do not give me anything, even if I beg you:
The love that I nurture for you has no need of hope.
Amen.

SAINT TERESA OF AVILA

Appendix 1
THE PENITENT MAGDALENE

The Penitent Magdalene / Michelangelo Merisi (Caravaggio)

A look of contemplation

In the Gospel of John (20:11–18), Mary Magdalene is convinced that she is speaking to the gardener, but when called by him with her name, "Mary!" she "turns," and discovers that it is Jesus.

Mary recognizes his voice and his presence.

It is especially here that we see evidence of the importance of having a personal encounter with the Lord: faith.

The Gospel of John begins to proclaim the identity between Jesus and his words. He himself is the Word, the Son, the revealer of the Father. Saying his name makes light come to the darkness buried in the heart.

Love is the principle of faith and recognition. One believes and knows that which he loves. Almost as if letting scales of blindness fall from one's eyes (like Saint Paul in Acts 9:18), the conversion that is born from listening to the word of the risen Jesus gives back the sight of faith.

The conversion experience of Mary Magdalene is represented with spontaneity and charm by a well-known painter, Caravaggio.

His real name is Michelangelo Merisi, called Caravaggio. He was born around 1571 in Milan.

With a fiery temperament and easily provoked to anger, he paints masterpieces that are rejected by many critics because he lies outside of the mainstream.

But in many of his paintings on religious subjects, we find a profound breath of light and peace.

Caravaggio has accomplished, among so many other works, a painting titled "The Penitent Magdalene (1594-1595)" that can be found in Rome in the Gallery *Doria, Pamphilj.*

The canvas presents a young girl seated on a chair in a room while she dries her long hair. On the floor there is a vase of perfume with precious stones scattered on the ground in an act of renunciation.

Set your vision somewhat to the side. The cheeks, the collar, the bosom, the blouse, the garment drawn up to her knees, the skirt of floral damask—all emphasize the simplicity and sweetness of her whole figure.

A few simple elements characterize the domestic intimacy of the painting.

Her repentance is very expressive. Her tears of pain over her past life are loaded with hope. Mary Magdalene is represented in the moment in which grace has touched her heart. Touched by grace (symbolized by the light that pours in on the left), Mary finally undresses herself of her old life. Rejected is the love that has no more power to fill up the emptiness of her heart. That which enchants is the position of her arms that seem to gather up and caress a new creature that is about to be born and at the same time is already born, a new life, beautiful, luminous, and pure.

The picture alludes to a love which the Lord has filled in her, a love which has permitted her to go away in peace.

To be simply one's self

For this she is ready. She is already divested of her earrings, her string of pearls, of every ornament. She has no further use of perfume. Even her hair is no longer given much care. It is loose and covers her shoulders.

Without these things, Mary is able to be simply herself before others, before herself and above all before God. From the cry of repentance and from her conversion is born a new Mary, simple and true, like the light that tears away the darkness from the dark room (and from her past life) and is tender and strong like the voice of the Master that has called her back to the life of grace.

This is the truth about all conversions: He who lives closed in on self, selfishly searching for himself and of his own success, cannot resist when touched by grace. He ceases to seek anxiously his own realization to finally rest, bare and sincere, under the glance of God. The condition is that one listen to the voice of the Risen One calling his name with love.

Appendix 2

WOMEN AT THE SERVICE
OF THE GOSPEL

General Audience of Pope Benedict XVI
Wednesday, February 14, 2007

Dear Brothers and Sisters,

Today we have come to the end of our journey among the witnesses of early Christianity mentioned in the New Testament writings. And we use the last step of this first journey to dedicate our attention to the many female figures who played an effective and precious role in spreading the Gospel.

In conformity with what Jesus himself said of the woman who anointed his head shortly before the Passion: "Truly I tell you, wherever the good news is proclaimed in the whole world, what she has done will be told in remembrance of her" (Matthew 26:13; Mark 14:9), their testimony cannot be forgotten.

The Lord wants these Gospel witnesses, these figures who have made a contribution so that faith in him would grow, to be known, and their memory kept alive in the Church. We can historically distinguish the role of the first women in early Christianity, during Jesus' earthly life and in the events of the first Christian generation.

Jesus, as we know, certainly chose from among his disciples twelve men as Fathers of the new Israel and appointed them "to be with him, and to be sent out to proclaim the message" (Mark 3:14).

This fact is obvious; but, in addition to the Twelve, pillars of the Church and fathers of the new People of God, many women were also chosen to number among the disciples. I can only mention very briefly those who followed Jesus himself, beginning with the Prophetess Anna (see Luke 2:36–38), to the Samaritan woman (see John 4:1–39), the Syrophoenician woman (see Mark 7:24–30), the woman with the hemorrhage (see Matthew 9:20–22), and the sinful woman whose sins were forgiven (see Luke 7:36–50).

I will not even refer to the protagonists of some of his effective parables, for example, the housewife who made bread (see Matthew 13:33), the woman who lost the drachma (see Luke 15:8–10), the widow who pestered the judge (see Luke 18:1–8). More important for our topic are the women who played an active role in the context of Jesus' mission.

In the first place, we think spontaneously of the Virgin Mary, who with her faith and maternal labors collaborated in a unique way in our redemption to the point that Elizabeth proclaimed her "Blessed...among women" (Luke 1:42), adding: "Blessed is she who believed..." (Luke 1:45).

Having become a disciple of her Son, Mary manifested total trust in him at Cana (see John 2:5), and followed him to the foot of the cross where she received from him a maternal mission for all his disciples of all times, represented by John (see John 19:25–27).

Then there are various women with roles of responsibility who gravitated in their different capacities around the figure of Jesus. The women who followed Jesus to assist him with their own means, some of whose names Luke has passed down to us, are an eloquent example: Mary of Magdala, Joanna, Susanna and "many others" (see Luke 8:2–3).

The Gospels then tell us that the women, unlike the Twelve, did not abandon Jesus in the hour of his passion (see Matthew 27:56, 61; Mark 15:40). Among them, Mary Magdalene stands out in particular. Not only was she present at the passion, but she was also the first witness and herald of the Risen One (see John 20:1, 11–18).

It was precisely to Mary Magdalene that Saint Thomas Aquinas reserved the special title, "Apostle of the Apostles" (*apostolorum apostola*), dedicating to her this beautiful comment: "Just as a woman had announced the words of death to the first man, so also a woman was the first to announce to the Apostles the words of life" (*Super Ioannem, ed. Cai*, 2519).

Nor was the female presence in the sphere of the primitive Church in any way secondary. We will not insist on the four un-named daughters of Philip the "Deacon" who lived at Caesarea; they were all endowed with the "gift of prophecy," as Saint Luke tells us, that is, the faculty of intervening publicly under the action of the Holy Spirit (see Acts 21:9). The brevity of information does not permit more precise deductions.

It is rather to Saint Paul that we are indebted for a more ample documentation on the dignity and ecclesial role of women. He begins with the fundamental principle for the baptized: "There is no longer Jew or Greek, there is no longer slave or free, there is no longer male and female; for all of you are one in Christ Jesus" (Galatians 3:28), that is, all are united in the same basic dignity, although each with specific functions (see 1 Corinthians 12:27–30).

The apostle accepts as normal the fact that a woman can "prophesy" in the Christian community (1 Corinthians 11:5), that is, speak openly under the influence of the Spirit, as long as it is for the edification of the community and done in a dignified manner.

Thus, the following well-known exhortation: "Women should be silent in the churches" (1 Corinthians 14:34) is instead to be considered relative. Let us leave to the exegetes the consequent, much-discussed problem of the relationship between the first phrase—women can prophesy in churches—and the other—they are not permitted to speak; that is, the relationship between these two apparently contradictory instructions. This is not for discussion here.

We already came across the figure of Prisca or Priscilla, Aquila's wife, who surprisingly is mentioned before her husband in two cases (see Acts 18:18; Romans 16:3): In any case, both are explicitly described by Paul as his *sun-ergoús*, "collaborators" (Romans 16:3).

There are several other important points that cannot be ignored. It should be noted, for example, that Paul's short Letter to Philemon is actually also addressed to a woman called "Apphia" (see Philemon 2). The Latin and Syriac translations of the Greek text add to this name "Apphia," the appellative "*soror carissima*" (ibid.), and it must be said that she must have held an important position in the community at Colossae. In any case, she is the only woman mentioned by Paul among those to whom he addressed a Letter.

Elsewhere, the Apostle mentions a certain "Phoebe," described as a deaconess "of the Church at Cenchreae," the port town east of Corinth (Romans 16:1–2). Although at that time the title had not yet acquired a specific ministerial value of a hierarchical kind, it expresses a true and proper exercise of responsibility on the part of this woman for this Christian community. Paul recommends that she be received cordially and assisted "in whatever she may require." Then he adds: "for she has been a benefactor of many and of myself as well."

In the same epistolary context the Apostle outlines with delicate touches the names of other women: a certain Mary, then Tryphaena, Tryphosa and "the beloved" Persis, as well as Julia, of whom he writes openly that they have "worked hard among you" or "worked hard in the Lord" (Romans 16:6, 12a, 12b, 15), thereby emphasizing their strong ecclesial commitment.

Furthermore, in the Church at Philippi two women were to distinguish themselves, Euodia and Syntyche (see Philippians 4:2). Paul's entreaty to mutual agreement suggests that these two women played an important role in that community.

In short, without the generous contribution of many women, the history of Christianity would have developed very differently.

This is why, as my venerable and dear predecessor John Paul II wrote in his apostolic letter *Mulieris Dignitatem*: "The Church gives thanks for each and every woman....The Church gives thanks for all the manifestations of the feminine 'genius' which have appeared in the course of history, in the midst of all peoples and nations; she gives thanks for all the charisms which the Holy Spirit distributes to women in the history of the people of God, for all the victories which she owes to their faith, hope, and charity: she gives thanks for all the fruits of feminine holiness" (n. 31).

As we can see, the praise refers to women in the course of the Church's history and was expressed on behalf of the entire Ecclesial Community. Let us also join in this appreciation, thanking the Lord because he leads his Church, generation after generation, availing himself equally of men and women who are able to make their faith and baptism fruitful for the good of the entire Ecclesial Body and for the greater glory of God.

[Source: http://www.vatican.va/holy_father/benedict_xvi/ audiences/2007/documents/hf_ben-xvi_aud_20070214_en.html.]